THE UNBELIEVABLE BELIEVABLE

More Tales from The Baron

BILLY J. BARNUM

Copyright © 2022 Billy J. Barnum

All rights reserved

First Edition

First originally published by Billy J. Barnum 2022

ISBN 9780578385167 (Paperback)

ISBN 9798201815608 (Digital)

Author's signature page

My Bleeding Heart

My bleeding heart, it bleeds for you

In everything I say and do

The world is harsh and wears you down

Now don't you dare now wear that frown

A little child is bald without choice

It's like he's never had a voice

A valiant man he has no legs

By one small step on a powder keg

And the man on tv tweets way too much

I'm sure that's just his injustice crutch

Plastic bottles choke the beast

It's like Satan's dining and having his feast

But no one's coming, where's superman?

To save the day, so what's the plan?

Just hold your breath 'til you turn blue

My bleeding heart it bleeds for you.

A Man and His Circus

P.T. Barnum the profiteer

Just play the music loud so they can hear

No penny to pay? Oh! what a sin

Maybe then you pay with your skin

Or do you have a deformed aunt?

Oh no, I shouldn't, oh no I can't!

Or is your father way too tall?

Strike up the band I'll take it all

When you enter

Through the doors

You'll be screaming

Out for more

I said strike up the band

And send in the clowns

Now go on the tight rope

And don't let me down

Is that a whisker?

I see on your chin

Oh where now, oh where now

Should I even begin

Continued...

Your mother is beautiful

She's 1200 pounds

Oh nickels and pennies

I'm hearing the sounds

Of a man and his jingle

And the humbug of night

Away on his elephant

He rides out of sight

This one's for you

I usually do it for myself

Without a worry in mind

I search, I look, I gaze upon

The many treasures I find

But, today I woke up feeling funny

Not a thing for myself I did not do

Oddly enough today what I did

Is I did this one for you

No selfishness, no self-control

Unhinged and often impulsive

Guided by an unknown force

Well this is sometimes how we live

As the day was done and the world was one

Not one moment was wasted feeling blue

Because of what it felt like

To do this one for you.

Depravity

Deprave, deprave, depravity

What an evil way to be

When all is wrong and nothing's right

Then cast away until daylight

And castaway upon my will

The hardest part is to be still

It eats you up no end in sight

And yields to me oh whoa the night

It curls itself up like a ball

Just waiting, and watching until you fall

A smirk of a smile is all you've got

And empty thoughts have he have naught

Scraping, clawing, bleeding inside

Untangled, unhinged, the seed of a bride

The demon that's living inside my brain

Numb and obnoxious and free from pain

He creeped in somewhere in the night

And never left, he evaded sight

No one saw him, no one cared

So he ran rampant and with no fear

Continued...

Taking all that he could take

Breaking every rule to break

Stopping nowhere, no end in sight

A vision of evil, a glorious sight

Courage is little and courage is earned

Courageous is he that accepts to be burned

And lives with the scars that is left on himself

A master of disguise, puts the book on its' shelf

It can rest, gather dust, leave a stain on the spill

Clean it up, gather strength, put its' name on a pill

For it won't be too long till it comes back again

When it does, do be warned that you won't call it friend

Deprave, deprave, depravity

What an evil way to be

When all is wrong and nothing's right

Then cast away until daylight

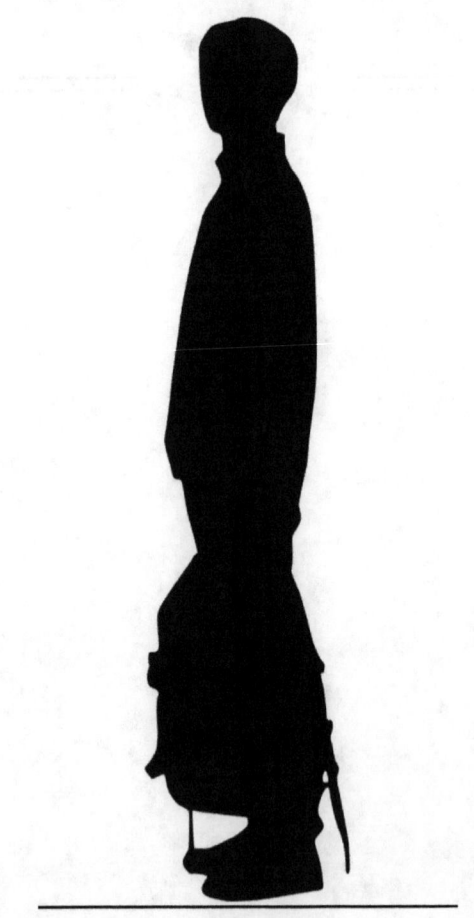

Tumbleweed

Tumbleweed they call me

Cause I drift from town to town

Never staying one place too long

Never settling down

Drifter's such a funny word

Don't you get it? Get my drift?

Like an opal wedged within

Through the sands I'll sift

Someday I may just plant my feet

But, I don't just know when

It's getting late I have to run

The clock is striking ten

The time has come for wanderin'

Like a feather flying high

Just like I told you, that's me

And that you can't deny

Will I miss what I might miss?

Or maybe make a memory I can't replace

Or maybe see in others

A precious solitude face

Continued...➤

A gust of wind, she lifts me up

And then I roll away

No longer being stationary

Watch me go! Away! Away!

A Twisted Mind

Pay a nickel for your thoughts

I'll sit right down; I think I ought

For do not fear, for what you'll find

A troubled soul, and twisted mind

It thinks of things

You don't desire

And it just might

Set stars on fire

A nova bright

In black of night

It turns with rings

Inside it stings

And hurts like hell

Then starts to swell

It then subsides

I know, it hides

And all this from

a twisted mind

Did you? Would you?

Expect to find

Pay for Electric?

When life gets busy

And things get hectic

Do I really have to

Pay for electric?

They could setup some windmills

Or solar if they tried

But instead they'd rather

Suck your wallet dry

A life's precious moment

A memory not forgotten

My electric bill grows bigger

To the core oh! how rotten!

If you're a pauper

You sit by candlelight

Lead a charmed life

A chandelier will light your night

Mom where's the lights?

Son where's the money?

Bees in the hive

Make a whole lot of honey

Continued...

A firefly will flicker

And light your yard for free

But not those little bastards

They'll jack it up times three

The night is growing long

And it's becoming quite too hectic

But just one question lingers on

Do I really have to pay for electric?

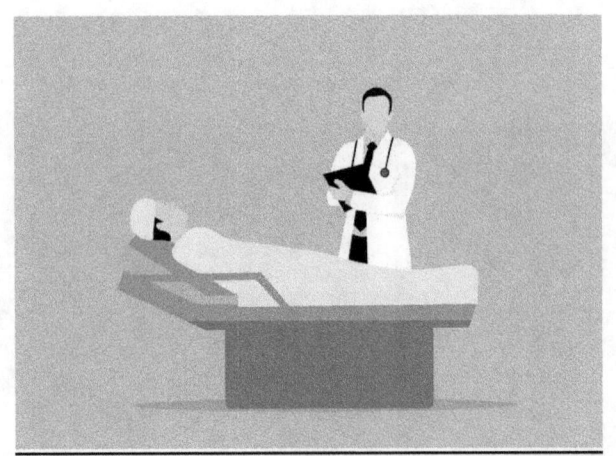

The Gift

Someone just gave

This man a gift

They said to him

Now you shall live

He sang his heart out

With resounding glee

But it just did not

Set him free

He carried on

And carried tunes

Which brought him to

The month of June

He left the coast

And moved to Maine

He missed his son

It brought him pain

He then picked up

A brush and pallet

And stroke by stroke

What should he call it?

Continued...

Shakespeare theater

Brick by brick

He found his passion

And this is it

And now he sits

Upon the trees

His destined canvas

With falling leaves

And rolling thunder

With mysterious skies

Mike has that twinkle

In his eyes

Baby

She's fast as lightning

When she takes a sniff

As I often wonder to myself

What if?

She could talk

What would she say?

All day long

She likes to play

She scratches the carpet

As I start to yell

She's mostly good

But, sometimes she's hell

She lands on her feet

When she jumps off the porch

She's the queen of the house

There's no passing the torch

Sometimes I call her Sheba

But her real name is Baby

She's a handful at times

When she's driving me crazy

Continued...

She stares, and she stares
Until you give her some food
If you don't then watch out!
She's in some kind of mood

She's fast as lightning
When she takes a sniff
As I often wonder to myself
What if?

She could talk
What would she say?
It would be
A crazy day

And then I think
And I wonder how
As she stares at me again
And says "Meow!"

Father Panik

When I was younger

There was a place called "Father Panik"

I'd hardly ever go there

Because my skin was too white

You'd get beat up in the daytime

You'd get killed there at night

They'd say, "Boy what you doing here?"

Didn't yo mama teach you better

Better pray to your god

Better send it in a letter

Man you must be crazy

Coming down this part of town

Coming with your cracker friends

In this gritty part of town

I said man "Why can't we just live as one?"

And see through all this haze

He said boy bess you better know

That racism runs both ways

Now get while the gettin's good

And don't come back no mo'

They ignorance is bliss

And now they know the score

Seasons

He said in the winter of my life

I was awoken by a dream

I can't interpret what it meant

I don't know what it means

But it was cold, so bitter cold

Knuckles numb I lost my grip

Lying broken on the ground

And just in my vision, the place where I slipped

He said in the springtime of my life

Flowers bloomed and butterflies flew

A new beginning, a glorious time

Like everything was all brand new

This is where he met his sweetheart

Flowing hair and sparkling eyes

She kissed him once then disappeared

Just before she removed her disguise

He said in the summer of my life

There was a beach and ocean shores

And horseshoe crabs and starfish

He couldn't want for anything more

Continued...

A beautiful mermaid, she comes from the sea

She holds out her hand, with a grip like thunder

He reaches out to grab it

And just like that he's going under

He said in the autumn of my life

Leaves turned colors such a beautiful hue

And time felt so precious

For just a remaining few

They found his body under a mountain of leaves

Gripped in his hand was a note that read:

"Through the seasons of my life

I lived them all and without strife

Now go live yours and do the same

Not a single regret I do not blame"

The Maestro

I'm the maestro

Watch me twirl

My wrists around

They swish and swirl

That man there

Wants to fall from line

With one quick point

And all is fine

Now keep the beat

And crash those cymbals

Up on your feet

You must be nimble

Everyone's like marionettes

And I "The puppet master" pull the strings

They sway to and fro all as one

Yes this is what I bring

Some say I'm mad

Some not so much

Yes you can look

But do not touch!

Continued…

Now keep the time

And keep the beat

And everyone back up

On your feet

For I'm the maestro

You must obey

And all the listeners

Will have a glorious day

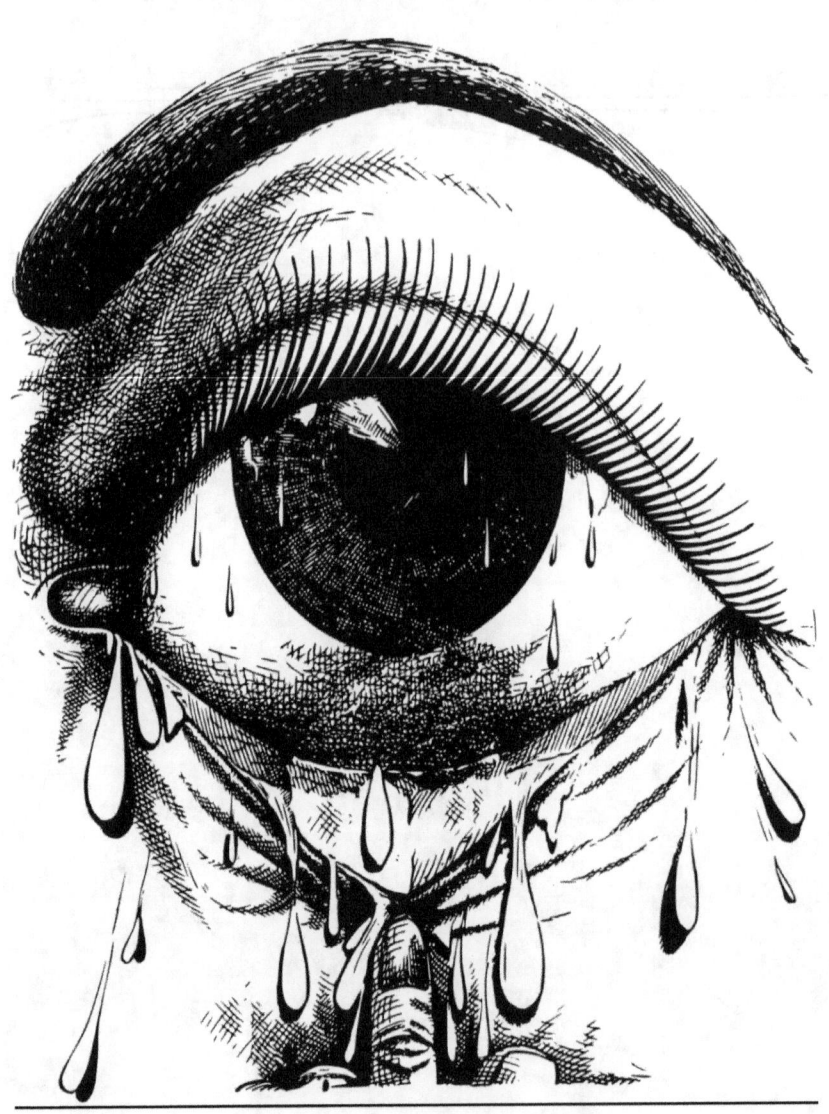

I'll wait for you

When distance seems to get too far

And hope is hanging from a star

When all seems lost without a clue

Till time runs out, I'll wait for you

When mountains fall

I'll wait for you

When eagles call

I'll wait for you

Digging trenches just to hide

10 yards away bombs collide

Around your neck you hold it true

Inscribed on a heart "I'll wait for you"

Days seem like months

And months seem like years

And when I lay my head to sleep

It's your voice that I hear

One day I awoke

To a knock at the door

The soldiers salute

Then the tears start to pour

Continued...

It feels like a dagger

Going straight through my heart

But the necklace had stopped it

Before it could start

As you stood at the gate

You refused to go through

As you promised in life

Your words have rung true

When distance seems to get too far

And hope is hanging from a star

When all seems lost without a clue

Till time runs out, I'll wait for you

I'll wait for you

I'll wait for you

I'll wait for you

I'll wait for you …

The Rocking Chair

Deep within my rocking chair

I rock here black as night

With crumpled hopes of what shall be

Uncrumpling back to life

Will it be just as it was

Before it rolled up like a ball

Or should we all just start to run

The voices start to call

The eyelids roll back in its' head

And then you dare to take a look

Feeling empty wondering

Not realizing just what it took

The keeper always guards the gate

Just who the hell does he think he is?

Your soul is held on by a string

If you play nice, he'll let you live

Dirty deeds are always done cheap

For just a penny to pay

Now sit back in your rocking chair

And all the rest better start to pray

Continued...

The night got dark

The moon it swells

And in the distance

You hear the bells

By the time you gasp for breath

By the way it didn't care

The sands of time have all run out

Impending doom, the rocking chair

Freak

They pushed and shoved him

Never loved him

The bullies pummeled

And fist and gloved him

They called him coward

Nerd and geek

They treated him

Just like a freak

They spit and threw

All that they could

They cursed and slandered

And beat him with wood

You know there's only

So much one man can take

Their eyes grew big

As he started to break!

He pulled out his Ouija

And casted his spell

By the look in his eyes

He seen remanence of hell

Continued...➡

"Bring hell to earth

And make them pay

But let them live

To see another day"

He repeated over and over again

For the rest of existence he wanted revenge

"I am not a freak that you made me to be"

Though your wish did come true, now rain down misery

Let sleeping dogs lie

Or consequences may come

Breathe in and breathe out

We should all live as one

Toilet Paper Pandemic

I went to the store

To get some toilet paper

But it seemed to disappear

Like a cloud of smoke vapor

So I drove down the road

And walked into another

The aisles were bare

"I said holy mother!"

So I decided to go home

And get some online

It was $20 per roll

Are you out of your mind?

Last week the stores were stocked

And now the shelves are bare

Where the hell did the toilet paper go?

I can't find it anywhere

I just have to find some

Before I go to the John

Or I'll be using a newspaper

My T-shirt or some yarn

Continued…

It's like toilet paper

Is now the new crack

As I sit on my throne

Waiting for it to come back

Fantasy

Sick of sickles

Trickling down

Fantasy

She wears a frown

Under the silo

Where it all began

Fantasy

She has no plan

On a trajectory

That's shooting straight up

Fantasy

Has an empty cup

And here it comes now

Smashing down

Fantasy

She is tossed to the ground

And when she feels

Like giving up

Fantasy

Takes a blow to the gut

Continued...

Someday maybe

Things can change

Fantasy

She's the queen of pain

And someday maybe

The stars will align

Fantasy

On your flesh will they dine

Thinking long

And thinking hard

Fantasy

Draws her name on a card

It's inside you

And inside me

Fantasy

Will set you free

Transient Tale

She wakes up crying in the night

Muttering these words half asleep

Repeating over and over again

"I pray the lord my soul to keep"

And in the distance the radio's playing

As she begins to tell her tale

She looks at me and then I hear

"Turn a whiter shade of pale"

Her face shifted shape

Then she starts to look mean

In the background I hear

"in a coat he borrowed from James Dean"

With a growl in her voice

I begin to move back

And wouldn't you know it

I hear "Back in black"

Her tale is haunting, eerie and weird

Now it's fight or flight I cannot lie

And at that moment I hear

"Goodbye my friend it's hard to die"

Continued...➡

She starts to sleepwalk

As I'm frozen in fear

She arrives at the radio

And all that I hear

Is "I will try to fix you"

As she smashes it down

Then awakes from her stupor

With an unknowing frown

The white of my knuckles

From gripping the bed

As the blood begins to flow

Turn pink and then red

She then starts to smile

And goes back to sleep

Muttering these words

"I pray the lord my soul to keep"

Epitaph

Hath not now this a rainbow

Whose colors shine so brightly

A million dreams all swirled inside

A fist that's clenched so tightly

We pulled and grabbed

It's not enough

To get the fist

To open up

Hoarding like a greedy thief

Not relenting, not one bit

Longing for our futures yearning

Feeling lost like this is it

A thousand lifetimes, a million souls

Asking now could this be over

And these three wishes that we've had

Windswept in an instance was our four-leaf clover

Blinding lights intensify

My brain it hurts, can't do the math

And all that's left, all that remains

A broken hollow epitaph

Birth of a Poem Continued

Words are written on the page

But I know the poem is not done

Then I hear a voice inside my head

Say "You dear sir are the chosen one"

Oh! My god

There it goes again

As I grab my notebook

And I grab my pen

Back to the blurred visions

And scribbling ensues

As I see all the colors

A multitude of hues

As I write along frantic

Like my house is on fire

I hear "Finish my work,

You're doing great dear sire"

Feeling exhausted

Like I've no more to spend

With a burst of elation

As I get to the end

Continued...

The poem is finished

As my vision turns clear

And I shake my head quickly

And wiggle my ears

Now the moment is over

With a feeling of Zen

As I end with a period

And I rest down my pen.

Running out of Time

Do the flowers need the weeds?

Or the weeds need the flowers?

Choking grip so tightly now

At last the final hours

Some may choose the poison

Some go pluck, pluck, pluck

Some just care just enough

Some go what the fuck

Can we coexist

Turning water into wine

Gluttonous indefinitely

We're running out of time

One kills one

One kills the other

Have they no morals

And no respect for their mothers

I can't tell you how to live

I can just observe your actions

Lying in a kind of hell

All your lives are up in traction

Continued...

Helpless but still a stubborn lion

Nonconformity, the devil breathes

And all the trees that used to live

Now have lost their leaves

And all the roots

Are dying now

And millions watching

Jaws dropped wide open, utter WOW!

Nothing sacred

Nothing gained

Was it worth

A mountainous pain

Seepage always starts the fear

Watch it crumble when no one cares

Flowers or weeds, we've planted the seeds

Combustible universe, and we should have head

Stranded?

Stranded on an island

As you washed upon the shore

All the questions in your mind are

Just how will you endure

As of tales of old

Are the mysteries unknown

As the story goes

Though the wicked wind blows

It's as old as time itself

The one with the genie in the bottle

Man I couldn't believe my eyes

As it came at me full throttle

Amazing as it seems

It came with all the perks

Three wishes and all that good stuff

It now was time to do the work

You can wish for anything

The genie says as he starts laughing

Anything means anything

And I will make it happen

Continued...

First I wish for food

To nourish my body so I can survive

I eat until my belly's full

Thank god I'm still alive

Second I wish for health

My body's strong, fit as a fiddle

Just one more wish left as I start to panic

Please help me solve this magic riddle

I close my eyes and make my last wish

My last wish is for world peace

The genie looking stunned

Says by my command this one's done with ease

He said congratulations

You're still stranded

Doesn't this leave you

Empty handed?

You could have wished for a boat

You could have wished for a plane

You must be certifiable

You must be insane

Continued...

I said genie believe me

I'm rich beyond words

Now get back in your bottle

As I soar like a bird

Thousand-Year Storm

The sky broke open

And the rain poured down

People were swimming everywhere

Just trying not to drown

Next they heard the thunder

And the lightning was crashing down

Feeling apocalyptic

What's happening to this town?

Roofs were caving in

All their memories lost in floods

It's taken every piece of their soul

And now it wants their blood

They called it the thousand-year storm

But they've seen this six months ago

So how could they call it that?

And now the winds they start to blow

Leaving devastation

Ripping trees up from their roots

A thousand-year storm my ass!

I think that notion is kind of mute

Continued...

It took a day then it was over

Lives were lost ...

All that remained was a memory

Of what used to be and all the cost

Now we see that

Climate change is real

But nothing is changing

Hey man! What's the deal?

So they'll go back to their cushy homes

Tucked away all safe and warm

While we sit there staring at the sky

Awaiting the next thousand-year storm

Hit and Run

He was playing ball with his brother

Up against the house

Just a child so innocent

Exuberance then all went south

The ball it bounced into the road

The brother said just let it go

But he ran into the road to get it anyway

And what happened next you don't want to know

A car was speeding down the hill

And launched this little boy in the air

He landed a block and a half away

The driver sped off without a care

His father was home from Vietnam

And pounded a dent in the ambulance

With a puddle of blood surrounding his body

The situation was very intense

He broke all the bones in his little body

With years of rehabilitation he learned to walk

Within a few more years

He learned again just how to talk

Continued...

They never caught the driver

That changed this little boys' life

So the boy grew up and became an author

And he carried on, and he did write

This story here is very true

And letting go of the past has set him free

And if you're wondering who that little boy was

That little boy was me

My Legacy

He said dad, why do you write so much?

And do you think it's necessary?

I said son, what if everyone kept their words inside their heads

Now don't you think that would be scary?

The ink that bleeds upon the page

Flows so freely from my veins

These crypted words inside this book

Are just an ounce of poets' pain

If it stays hidden from daylight

Will it then be all in vain?

The scholars ponder and thirst for more

A masterpiece and freedoms stain

I beckon thee go on thy path

Released to the world it shall be freed

For all the words that I've written down

Shall now become my legacy

Cancer

It ravaged her body

And tore a hole in her heart

The chemicals and the chemo

Was a terrible start

Of what was to come

And the uncertainty

Of how this would end

Why can't this just let her be

She said "you don't know how strong you are

Until you have to stand up and fight"

As I had to watch her lie awake

And the cruelty she endured night after night

As the needles went in

And it coursed through her veins

Her disguise was a smile

Through the excruciating pain

As I held out my hand

To put hers inside mine

With positive thoughts and positive vibes

As I write this today she's still alive

Continued...

I guess you can say we both jumped in the ring

We fought with four hands instead of two

When you're put in this situation

You have to do, what you have to do

That evil cancer tried to take her away

But we wrapped her in prayers and kept her warm

Like a hero she wears a badge of courage

And a blue-ribbon tattoo inked on her arm

When Santa Claus is Coming

When Santa Claus is coming

The kids are fast asleep in bed

But that's just from a fairytale

From long ago that someone said

Truth be told they're wide awake

Fingers crossed under the sheets

Wishing, hoping, and praying

For all the toys they'll get to keep

The parents come to tuck them in

Their eyes are closed, and they pretend

That sugar plum fairies are dancing in their heads

But they're actually waiting for that special friend

Cheeks all red and rosy

Down the chimney they hear him bounce

They go to take a peek

But they're too late, they only see the reindeer pounce

Up, up and away, he's already gone

But they're still full of cheer

The Christmas tree is surrounded by presents

And there's a bite in the cookie it does appear

Continued...

So they go back to bed, and say all of their prayers

With the feelings of love cause their family is near

With the memories of reindeer taking off into flight

Merry Christmas to all, and to all a good night

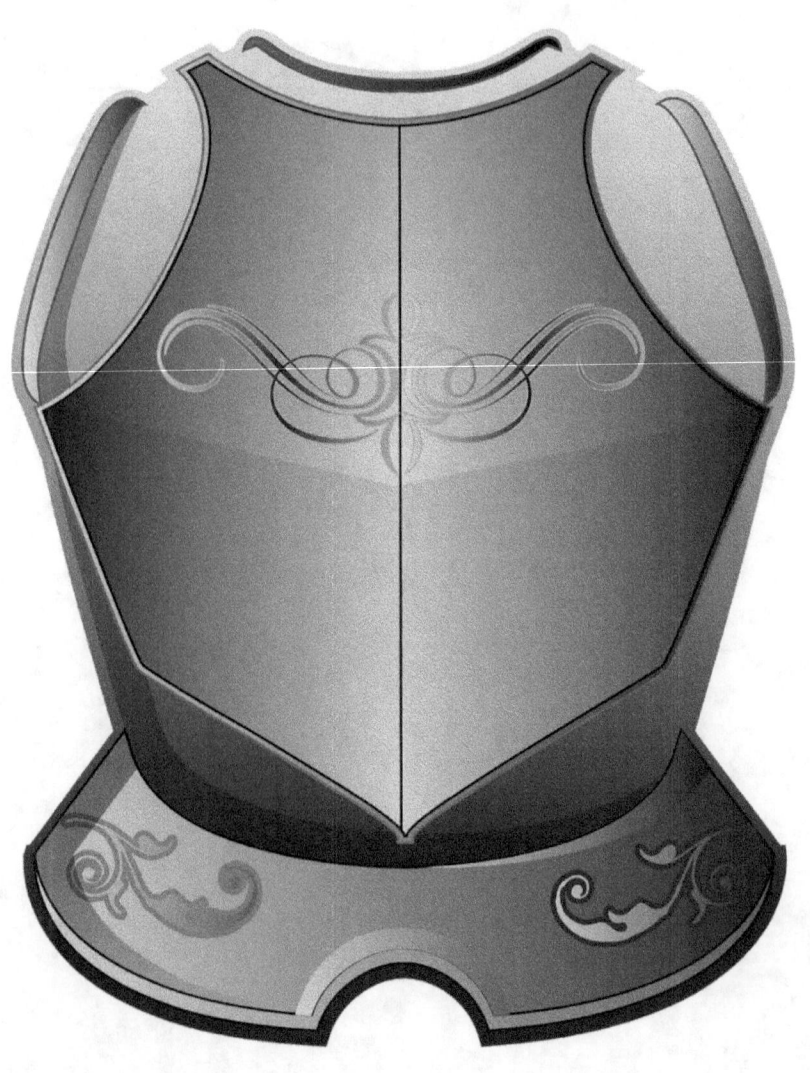

Bulletproof

I know you think I'm bulletproof

But I can assure you, that you're dead wrong

All the things that I have to say

I had to put it in a song

And then I wrote this poem

To thine self to be true

My armor's wearing thin now

As you see now I'm not so bulletproof

But you can win a thousand arguments

Telling everyone that I am

And how you worship every step

Of this broke down superman

A figment of my imagination

I rush to the closet and put on my suit

And then the cape, and then the gloves

A powerful wreck, now ain't that cute

I fly away and out of sight

Way up high above the roofs

and all the while your mind's made up

that you still think I'm bulletproof

Merry-Go-Round

Through my life I've been on a merry-go-round

I flew up in the air and then came right back down

There was always that one horse that never did move

Like he didn't fit in and just lost his groove

Stationary is not such a bad place to be

Even though you're not moving you still can be free

While the others are floating and touching the stars

Be confident and courageous and know who you are

Belittle is little importance to you

Find the worth in your pride and just do what you do

When the judgement starts coming and it takes all you have

And your feet are in quicksand and all does seem bad

You just march up the steps and bang on the door

You're a triumph in waiting and destined for more

The lights will shine brightly on your presence they'll shone

From the day you were born you felt it in your bones

Now spread your wings and never look down

It is now time for you to get off this merry-go-round

Season of Dread

Reaper of night, and reaper of day

He comes out with the jester who's ready to play

Who's all decked out with his silly balled hat

As he conjures up spells from rabies filled bats

As the tentacles reach much far beyond realm

With the duo of havoc taking over the helm

As they crash, pillage, and plunder for the sake of delight

The unstoppable disaster for the king of the Reich

The bigger the shield, the harder they fall

As the screams fall on deaf ears of unanswerable calls

One last ounce of hope with triumph waiting in the wings

If good doesn't come, then it's unimaginable things

The scene has been set as anticipation wears thin

To the victor go the spoils in this lopsided chagrin

Pulling the covers up over their heads

As the battle continues in this season of dread

Begins Again

We start out small and learn to walk

And then for most, we learn to talk

Some play with dolls, some play with trucks

For some it's great, for some it sucks

Some will eat from a golden spoon

And some will march to a different tune

We'll keep our manners as we go through school

As teachers teach us the golden rule

Once school is through some go to war

Some make lots of money and want more, more, more!

Then some come home bursting with pride

As others start questioning just why they're alive

For the lucky ones they get to grow old

To their grandkids a lifelong story is told

The ones that believe close their eyes and say when

With their last breath, and then their first, it all begins again

We Shall Carry On

I curse the past of pendulant

Through knee deep snow the forest danced

The bouncy moon how high it bounced

The wolf in tears on prey it pounced

On days of sorrow, on days of gay

On knees bent backwards, on knees it prays

Oh! Scary thoughts they paint a muse

Indignity straight up in choose

Parts seas, and bees sting oh so well

Embroidered, stitched, a patterned swell

Come hither he stares with star struck eyes

American vengeance and the napalm shall fly

Crafts fears out of courage and doubt be gone

For the sake of our people we shall carry on

How Will They Remember Me?

Did you ever think to yourself
How will they remember me?
And did you ever think they'd say
He lived his life so wild and free

He did some crazy stuff
Just a step before the edge
And sometimes he seemed to teeter
But kept his balance up on the ledge

He lived his life with passion
And kept his ducks all in a row
Some places I wouldn't think of going
He said, "what the hell" and he would go

Courage laced with bravery
Hardnosed mixed with nice
Bold and brash and in between
Sugar mixed with spice

Sometimes I wonder when I'm all alone
Me and my heartbeat wondering who I could be
And the thought that crosses my mind is
Just how will they remember me?

The Last Train to Nowhere

We grabbed our tickets and climbed aboard

It was the last train to nowhere or so we had heard

As the whistle rang out I heard an infant cry

We counted our pennies and prayed to the sky

This rhythmic thunder started slow then pounded fast

As light turned to night on peoples faces shadows were cast

The baroness landscape made some ominous with fear

As it chugged along the bridge over water a woman wept fallout tears

The attendant came through saying "Would you like a snack?"

That's when we all knew there was no turning back

In suitcases packed tight were people's hopes and their dreams

But would it be worth going through any means

It was the last train to nowhere that's what we were told

And at the end we'd be richer than silver and gold

Too Serious

I climbed up the mountain just to see the sunrise

But when I arrived I got a surprise

The sun wasn't shining there was nothing but rain

Cause the old man was crying, his heart was in pain

With a tear in his eye and a staff in his hand

As he points to the desert draws a line in the sand

There are two sides you see; one is evil one is good

As the battle rages on, no surrender, no one would

And not on my kingdom where there once was so plenty

They've depleted it all and now there's not any

For thirst there is fire and unthinkable things

On thy fingers I have bled to covet thy rings

Now back to the mountain where the sun doesn't shine

And the clouds holding memories that once used to be mine

As he pounds down his staff mighty lions they roar

And they all disappear as the clouds start to pour

Rock Star

I waited fifteen damn hours

Just to get on that stage

And by the look at the crowds faces

I was an anxiety rage

As lights shot out of the rafters

My wept guitar was really mean

People were dancing amazingly crazy

Getting lit up by colored light beams

It was like a train rolling faster

Going loop-the-loop on a roller coaster

Trying to hold on to what's in your pockets

Yeah I walked in real shy, but now watch me bolster

As I jumped up on the Marshall Stacks

I started playing "God of Thunder"

As the crowd went ballistically wild

I went up and down and all around and now I'm going under

The most wildest night of my life

I sat up and then I screamed

Rubbed my eyes, then looked in the mirror

It was the night of my life, and it was only just a dream

Under the Windmill

Under the windmill we danced, and we played

While marionette's put on a show in a glorious way

While sprinkles of magic dust fell on their heads

With a smile far left of sideways and not straight instead

Sugar plum gumdrops are gooey and sweet

Papa said to wear galoshes so not to get wet feet

I pardon thy favor as my partner did change

As we splashed and we frolicked it started to rain

The parade marches on not a drop did not spoil

As she stole me right back really slick just like oil

Nonsense makes some sense said a silly old fool

As we slipped from the windmill and fell in a pool

And the dept was just inches but I'm telling you now

We fell deeper and deeper then up to my brow

And our stories entangled just like wild déjà vu

I went back to the classroom and adjacent was you

There's a few special moments that you get in this life

And if you're lucky enough you just might get a wife

I held my toast gripped real tight being careful not to spill

As we danced and we played under the old windmill

Crash and Burn

It's time to crash and burn

And leave my blood out on this stage

These steel bars they cannot hold me

Like Houdini I broke out of this cage

If there's too many balls it's okay

I'll juggle every one

Life's too short to be mediocre

Straight to the stars I'm having too much fun

If you can achieve greatness

By just believing in your dreams

Why do you think they couldn't see it

Dancing shadows in moon beams

Are you the puppeteer

Or the puppet in the show?

Belief is all it takes

Only you will need to know

The afterglow is mighty

But is it mightier than the sword?

You chose the pen and paper

And you answered with your words

Continued...

So when they finally do applaud

Should you even acknowledge that they're there?

Or take a bow and leave the stage

And carry on without a care

You see sometimes when you crash and burn

It doesn't mean the flame has died

It means it burned so bright and hit the nebula

That ignited a spark so bright where stars collide

No one can touch you

But someday you'll come down

No matter how high you went up

Your feet were always on the ground

What if

What if it's just this

What if it's just now

What if hanging from a star

Was what if, no way!, how?

What if dreams were just no more

Just thoughts that crossed our minds

What if we never went to the moon

No imaginations or treasures to find

That's one small step for man

What ifs can be so cruel

Houston we're not coming home

We're running out of fuel

But what if we let ourselves go

And do whatever we please

And boldly go where no man's gone

Pulled up our bootstraps and got off our knees

Impart your wisdom for those who want it

For those who don't just walk on by

But what if you can change the world

Just by looking at the sky

Rhyme or Reason

I was panning for gold

And always ended up disappointed

I was stuck inside myself

Like I needed to be anointed

What if the next pan

Had an abundance of gold

Or what if I wasted all my years

On nothingness and it turns me old

Well you can't get back

Turn the hands of time

And you better make damn sure

That all your reasons rhyme

And all that glitters and sparkles

Doesn't always shine

Visions of grandeur may fill up your head

But the richest of men get to say "this is mine"

And no one can ever take it away

Cause they made up their mind and they earned it

The door that they chose took them out of that maze

An invaluable lesson and they learned it

Circles

They say life's a series of vicious circles

But some circles can be good

They say what comes around goes around

If you don't expect that, well maybe you should

They say you get what you give

And you give what you get

On a Tuesday in November

It might happen just yet

The queen sits upon her throne

Awaiting for everyone to bow

And they all do except one pauper

Oh! The look in her eyes like she's having a cow!

"You standing tall boy tell me your name"?

He said my name is William

She said "guards take him out of here

and give him a million"

The others stayed knelt and bowed

With the look on their faces of confusion

She said those who are bold enough to not fall in line

Will achieve the grand illusion

Continued…

And that man will pass his fortunes along

And so on, and so on, and so forth

Just a moment in time infused in the circle

And a man that changed his lineage by knowing his worth

Life of a Writer

A vision hit my mind

And I had to write it down

Like my head went under water

Then my thoughts started to drown

I felt a pain inside

Just like someone poked my spleen

Then I saw ghosts, and ghouls, and goblins

Man this must be Halloween

Standing at the edge

Of a volcano with molten lava

I wondered will I finally wake up

If I had a cup of java

Then I'm on a big jet plane

And we're heading towards the ground

Cockpit instruments going nuts

My head hits the pillow gently touching down

I know there's more to come

But that's it for today

The alarm clock starts to ring

And now I'm ready to face the day

Pass me by

He stands at the corner

With a cardboard sign in his hands

That reads "I'm hungry please help"

But most people don't understand

Cause they have food on their tables

And a nice house with warm heat

So they drive right by him

With no opportunity to meet

The husband says: he probably would have spent the money

On crack or some other drugs

The wife says: maybe he just needed food

Some conversation, and some love

As they head to their home

They keep thinking how familiar the man looked

Then like lightning it hits them

And their demeanor is shook

Do you remember right next door

The house that went into foreclosure?

That man with the sign was our neighbor

Then the tears start to flow as they lose their composure

Continued...

The moral of the story is

If it happened to him it can happen to you

Don't be so judgmental

And don't be so cruel

Treat everyone as equals

Have compassion for mankind

Be a good human being

And a more beautiful world you will find

An Epic Tale

An epic tale, an epic tale, an epic tale indeed

I toss about in tattered torn and then I start to bleed

Not native from I shall be one

A roaming rock near an extinguished sun

The hills they always run up oh so high

A dizzying depth with my head in the sky

Bamboo flavored licorice acts as a treat

As they stumble and trip up yeah that's just my feet

The young ones they run off telling truths, telling lies

As the Master of Students finally reveals his disguise

All this scribble and squabble don't be bringing me down

As the paint slowly fades away from the tears of a clown

An epic tale told for many generations

As it skips, leaps, and bounds through many a nation

There's no finding out seaside's slip from the slopes

And away in the bottle floats away all our hopes

Shine

By the shine of your soul

I can see it all so clear

By the astute of your attention

It is forcing me to hear

Sounds in life so intricate

Moving too fast, I missed it

A step behind I can't catch up

It's worth the cost, I risked it

A chance encounter

A blip in time

Just one moment

To catch that shine

I feel like I'm the chosen one

My lucky number, they come in threes

And perched upon my stoop so high

My hair is blowing in the breeze

I say, "God is this heaven?"

He says, "every day can be"

Now go and use your gift so wisely

And fulfill your destiny

26 Letters

It's just 26 letters

And that's all it is

And depending on the arrangement

It turns from mine to his

They line up all different

And can give you a house

They can steal your cheese

Run-away little mouse

They can bring you despair

And give you such bliss

They can give you a soulmate

And then give you a kiss

You can even arrange them

Anyway that you choose

And sometimes you'll win

And sometimes you'll lose

These 26 letters

Make up thousands of words

But be careful how you say them

Or you're bound to get burned

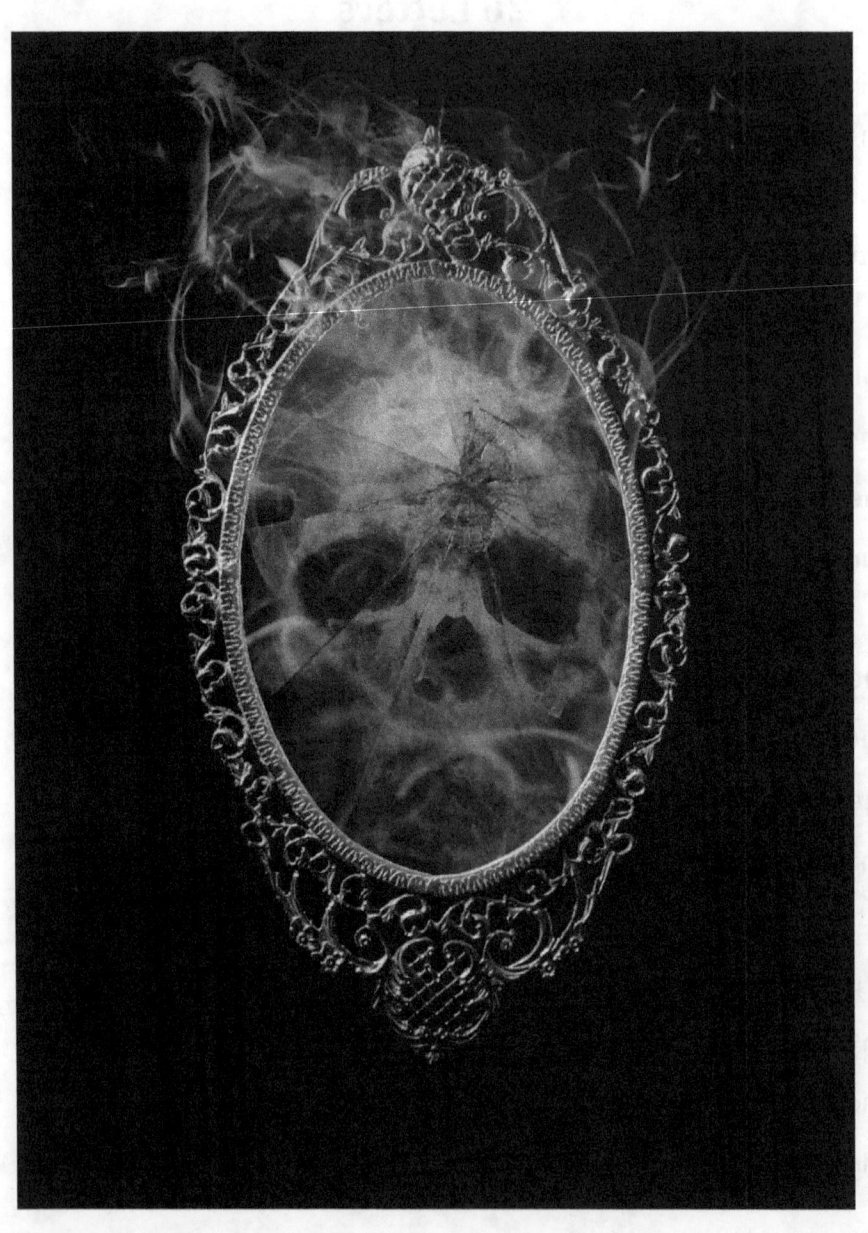

Blessing and a Curse

It's a blessing and a curse

That's how the old saying goes

The same thing that brings you joy

Might also bring you woes

You might win a large sum of money

Walking tall with spanking new boots

But twins may show their face

When evil grows its roots

You're a stunner and a saint

Always invited to the party

But soon your shit will start to stink

And will drive away your prince charming

Reflections in the mirror

Soon may change with brutal force

Stay humble, kind, and grounded

Hold the wheel and stay the course

And maybe all your blessings

Will be that and only that

Be the one you want to be

By only wearing just one hat

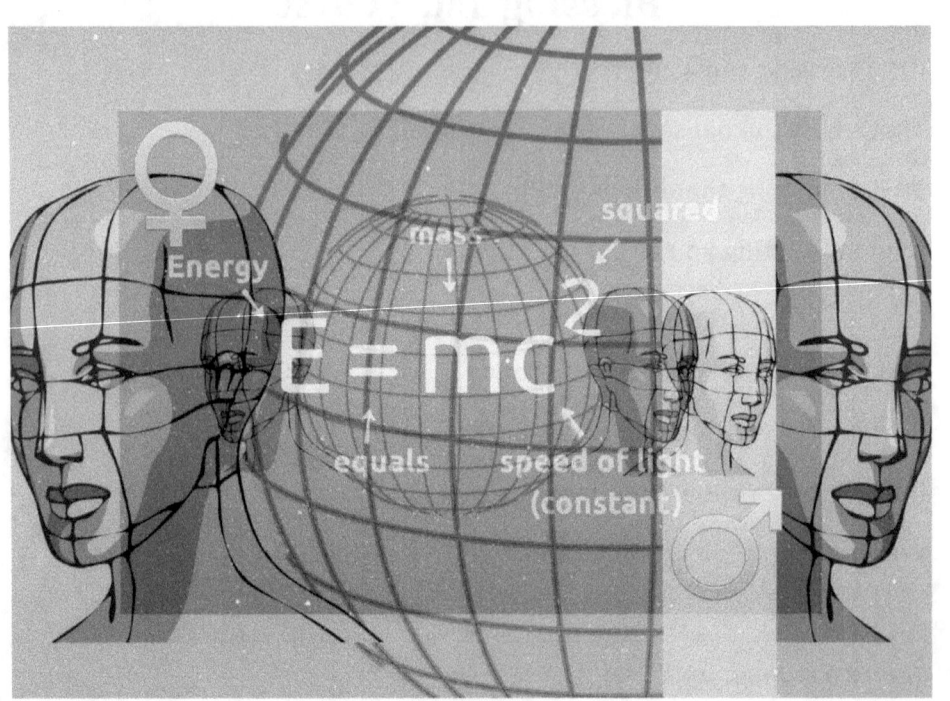

Accidental Einstein

Just one look

And that's when I knew

You'd be leaving my heart

All tangled and blue

She's got to be a Gemini

I could see it in her eyes

Flames burning, but cold as hell

Accidental Einstein was a part of her disguise

She hit me like a bus

No, maybe it was a truck

She said don't play the lottery today

Cause boy you're out of luck

Witchy woman with gray skull tendencies

She'd go off the charts all solar

My conscious said "I bet a thousand bucks"

That Medusa is bipolar

If you want your world turned upside down

Just go ahead and try it

If you got a kite, and feel the need

Just go ahead and fly it

Poem for the Fallen

When the time did come to step up

They did what they were asked

Digging trenches, following orders

They completed every task

They left behind their families

They left behind their lives

They left behind their husbands

They left behind their wives

No sacrifice too large

And no sacrifice too small

No remorse and no regrets

It's just sacrifice that's all

A common goal, a common vision

To be unified as one

And he who holds the golden torch

Of victory and battles won

Brother by brother, sister by sister

Arm in arm through the trenches they go

With pride in their hearts and a badge of courage

Is all they'll ever know

Time

Time is a precious thing

Some watch the clock; some hear it ticking

A mesmerizing metronome

Of standing still, a boot is kicking

What will you do with the time you have?

Will you be still with a foolish look?

Me, I'll savor every second

I think that I shall write a book

For you to read, or maybe millions

Then maybe time will not be wasted

You'll try a peach, a plum, a pear

You'll tell the tales of fruit's you've tasted

Then you'll leave the house and forget about time

And grow very old and wonder where time has gone

Then your thoughts will turn to visions

Like a lifelong movie playing from dusk to dawn

Rollercoasters and bumble bees

Cotton candy and starlit trees

Friends you've made, and friends who've passed

And times that have brought you to your knees

Continued..

But you'll always be thankful

Of the time you had

And the unwasted moments

That made you glad

And the memories are stories

For your children to carry on

A legacy of life

That you lived, when you're gone

The Last Poem

This is my last poem

Cause I have nothing left to write

But I hope that my words

Have helped your imagination take flight

We've been through the "Black Rose"

And "The Dream of the Lion"

And as sad as it seems

We've witnessed a tragedy as we've seen the clowns crying

We've seen "The Birth of a Poem"

And then we seen the birth of a poem end

And to all of my supporters

I am proud to call you my friends

We've seen "Crazy Skies"

And a "Purple Moon"

We've searched for "The Missing Piece"

Where "Serenity" looms

We've been "Alone in the Dark"

Where "All is Black"

And have heard a "Lonely Echo"

Where Jack knows it's not coming back

Continued..

Now with "Transient Tales"

And stories of "The Gift"

Across new horizons

I give you a lift

But don't be too sad

Cause if the elements are just right

An ember will form

And a spark will ignite

And the words will flow again

Just like water unto wine

And a whole new book of poems may be born

Like a true miracle of the divine

Free pictures provided by pixabay

Cover Design: SelfPubBookCovers.com/Island

I would like to thank everyone for your support. In the literary world without you there is no me.

Billy J. Barnum

If you like this book please check out my 1st book. Thank you again!

ABOUT THE AUTHOR

Billy J. Barnum is widely referred to as "The Simple Mans Poet" because he uses words that are easy to understand and that flow within his poetry. Unlike some other works where you have to stop mid-poem or story to look up a word in the dictionary or on Google. Genius is not figuring out how to squeeze as many adjectives or big words into a story but being creatively simplistic.

Since his first books release he still resides in Connecticut as a lifelong resident born and raised. He enjoys the beauty that Connecticut has to offer and loves the four seasons. He often talks to his close friends and relatives about the pride that he feels when he drives by the P.T. Barnum statue at Seaside Park in Bridgeport then tells stories about the "Greatest Showman on Earth" that his last name derives from. He is also very fond of the Barnum Museum.

It is believed that Billy J. Barnum started working on this the second book in the "Tales from the Baron" series shortly after the release of the first book as requests started pouring in asking for another. It is rumored that he wanted it to be more profound and have more wild tales in it so it could be cherished for generations to come. It is suggested that each person who owns and loves his books should pass this sentiment on to loved ones and friends so they can experience his one of a kind artistry for themselves as well.

(Photo taken by Orion Storm Barnum)

Dream Big!

www.ingramcontent.com/pod-product-compliance
Lightning Source LLC
Chambersburg PA
CBHW072335300426
44109CB00042B/1625